Skin Whispers Down

Hi dear Janice ~ what a
struggle it was - I'm so early
I say it apology and figuring
it all . Thank you for being
a quietly caring part of then.
Blessings to you + the
things
Love,
Marilyn

Skin Whispers Down

Marilyn Iwama

thistledown press

National Library of Canada Cataloguing in Publication Data

Iwama, Marilyn Joy, 1953-
Skin whispers down / Marilyn Iwama.
(New leaf editions. Series eight)
Poems.
ISBN 1-894345-65-7

I. Title. II. Series.
PS8567.W35S54 2003   C811'.6   C2003-911117-2

Cover photograph by Allison Muri
Book and cover design by J. Forrie
Typeset by Thistledown Press

Thistledown Press Ltd.
633 Main Street
Saskatoon, Saskatchewan, S7H 0J8
www.thistledown.sk.ca

Thistledown Press gratefully acknowledges the financial assistance of the Canada Council for the Arts, the Saskatchewan Arts Board, and the Government of Canada through the Book Publishing Industry Development Program for its publishing program.

ACKNOWLEDGEMENTS

To the Social Sciences and Humanities Research Council for support in the early stages.

To everyone at Sage Hill 2001, in particular: Marilyn Dumont, Warren Cariou, Betsy Warland and my fellow intro students.

To friends whose affections and commitment helped shape these poems.

For their gift of teaching: Sue Goyette, Rosalyn Ing, Alannah Young, Seepeetza Shirley Sterling and the writing class of '99. Laurie Ricou, for generously taking it all in stride and knowing when the time was right. Maria Campbell, for insisting on love.

To members of the Halifax writing groups for taking care.

To the Writers' Federation of Nova Scotia for making a home — especially Jane Buss — whose determination and grace created my opportunity. This volume was conceived during the Federation's first mentorship program. Sue MacLeod, for her example of respect and excellence.

To editorial staff where versions of some of these poems have appeared: *Prairie Fire*, CBC Radio One, *Grain*, *Journal of Mennonite Studies*, *Other Voices*. Some information and lines in "One Little Two Little" and "Giving Your Hand to a Halfbreed" are from *The Treaties of Canada with the Indians of Manitoba and the North-West Territories, Including the Negotiations on Which They Were Based*, Alexander Morris. Calgary: Fifth House, 1991, and *Sessional Papers* (No 11) 40 Victoria – A. 1877.

To the folks at Thistledown, and Judith Krause, editor and friend.

To the elders who freely shared their wisdom.

To my family, known or not, for the stories and love that make us. Clo and Gabrielle, for lines in "The Scattering." Mom and Uncle Bud, for such giving. Janis, for daring, for sharing her words and walking with me.

And to George, where the ocean meets the shore.

Thank you.

CONTENTS

For my sons
Adam Taro, Daniel Akihiro, Samuel Yasuhiro

SUBJECT: FAMILY

From: miwama@hotmail.com
To: jbrass@hall.com

thanks so much for returning my call. i wanted to talk, but i
was relieved that you weren't home — the message on your
machine sounded so confident, i couldn't see how we'd be
related.

then you call back and your first question is "are you native?"
and i think, "she's family all right." i mean, who else but
one of us would need some "stranger" to tell her what she is.

i can't wait to meet you. lifestream deli, six o'clock — right?

your cousin (can you believe it?!)
marilyn

QUESTIONS I WOULD ASK

Why do I see the girl and Wolf
on the crest of a sage-covered hill?
She leans into his shoulder as they gaze out
over jack pine and birch. Why do I feel
fur and muscle against my cheek
as I remember? The billow of his breath.

Why does a little person visit
when the pain in my chest stops
my breathing? She looks like
Grandma Caroline
in the palm of my hand.
Smoking her pipe and chuckling
pleurisy root and *sassafras*.

Why do I see Grandma Bella
in her calico dress and straw hat
teeter on the catwalk in a twilight theatre?
One arm gathers in daughter and
granddaughter. The other coils a circus rope.
Belly laugh ripples as she jumps. Why
is she telling their frightened eyes *lighten up?*
Back and forth.
Back and forth.

Why do I dream a flock of ravens
landing at my feet? A raven
an auburn haired woman who
leads me away by the hand.

Why does a wolf cross my path
as we drive home to the next funeral

too soon after the last?
Why does she wait until I reach her
before she walks into the forest?

Why doesn't anyone die old anymore?

Why do I dream
of naming ceremonies?
Nuns who look like me. Elders
who laugh at my mistakes.

SUBJECT: SLIP-UP

From: miwama@hotmail.com
To: jbrass@hall.com

sorry if i said too much last night, and about losing it. it's like there's a wall, holding it all in and then something happens — a word, a look. hearing about your childhood — all that stuff . . .

i can't stop thinking how our folks look like twins but act like they're from different families. you grow up fighting the whole "drunken indian" thing, i get to be the "blue-eyed blonde" throw-back of dedicated church-goers. mom must have been relieved when she saw me.

did i say too much?

worried,
m

_____

From: jbrass@hall.com
To: miwama@hotmail.com

no, of course you didn't. i'm sorry you're feeling as you are. i was worried that you were disappointed in *me*.

want to know my mantra? avoid feelings at all cost. if you can't, break the moment with humour — like my dad does. lock your feelings deep inside. we don't need any red flags waving.

i'm not trying to blame anyone, just recognizing where the patterns come from. and apologizing.

see why i was so relieved you agreed to write and not just do this in person, even though we live in the same city?

i'm still glad we've met.

love,
janis

Just say, for some reason, your grandma can't raise your mom
so your grandma leaves your mom with your great-grandma
and goes to the next province and marries some white guy
and has a whole other family. Just say you find out about all
this and you're really mad at your mom for not telling you
and you tell your mom how you've got rights too.

You find out where your grandma went and you go there and
your grandma's dead. You meet her husband and he's really
old and he's dying and right before he dies he tells you your
great-grandpa is your grandpa too. So you start asking your
dead grandma to tell you the truth.

Then say you find this great book by Maria Campbell and you
carry it around in your backpack for ages until one rainy after-
noon you sit in a pub like your grandma did, with a glass of
beer, and you read it. You read a story called "Jacob" about a
woman who finds out her dad is her husband's dad too. She
finds that out right when the priest is stealing her kids and in
all the noise and trouble nobody sees her go down to the river
and drown.

Say, right after you read that story, you go to class and you find
out Maria Campbell's coming that very day. When you go
around the circle saying who you are, she says she knows your
family. Then she reads that story out loud — the one called
"Jacob" that you just read.

After she's finished, she holds her book and you put yours in
your pack. You ride away on your bike in the wind and the
rain and the book burns into your back the whole way home.
Just say all that happened.

NOT ONE OF HER BETTER DAYS

You tell me
what the hell kind of person I'm supposed to be. Tell me
a name for blood that burns the skin
saying who is
who. Tell me.
Who's that in the mirror?
Tell me how I can be
with everyone around me
EVERYBODY thinking
I'm someone else
belonging to them and them
or not them oh no never them. Tell me
when my eyes are burning about this
or that someone dying
someone gone someone
lying to me about this and that
you tell me
what words
there are
to use.

SUBJECT: REUNION

From: miwama@hotmail.com
To: jbrass@hall.com

well, brother and sister are together again! i WISH you could
have come with us.

my dad, your mom, and i all trailed in to your dad's hospital
room behind mom. the two of them grabbed each other in a
huge hug — i.v. tubes and all — and burst into tears. we
waited for things to calm down a little, then the three of us
slipped out and left them alone.

45 years apart. what a shame.

later, we all congregated in the lounge. little brother and big
sister couldn't stop touching each other. your dad kept
patting mom's back and she kept stroking his hand around
the tubing.

the two of them talked like they were teenagers . . . uncle bud
(i love saying that!) teasing mom about her old boyfriends,
mom protesting, "oh bud, stop it," like she wanted him to go
on forever.

bringing them together was the right thing, wasn't it?

hoping,
m

Grandpa Peter wouldn't sign the treaty at Fort Qu'Appelle. Not when the governor invited us to open our hearts like children to a father. Not even when the governor said he couldn't believe we'd be the first Indians to refuse the hand of Our Mother the Queen. Coté and The Gambler were speaking for the Saulteaux. Loud Voice for the Cree. Grandpa Peter stood with the other headmen and listened to his brother George explain to all of them what the governor was saying.

The Gambler wouldn't buy it at first, especially when he saw how slow the governor was to accept the hand of a Halfbreed. *You were slow in giving your hand to a Halfbreed* The Gambler said through Uncle George. The governor started going on about that shootout with the Americans at Fort Pelly, how the queen protected us there and what a big help the Halfbreeds were to him last winter at Lake of the Woods, how he'd even told the queen that and the Indians shouldn't worry: Our Mother the Queen would be just and generous with the Halfbreeds.

The governor reminded The Gambler that he always spoke earnestly with a pure heart. If he was a little slow in taking Uncle George's hand, well, he just wasn't sure that Uncle George was authorized.

Buffalo were hard to find by then and a lot of us were dying. The governor promised he'd send some rations along. Grandpa Peter figured anything the government sent would likely be contaminated. And the governor *was* slow about shaking his brother's hand. Coté went ahead and signed. Grandpa Peter told the governor *no thanks.*

ARTIFACT

I stood inside a tipi for the first time today
at the Glenbow Museum. Remembered
someone saying

> *the grandmother*
> *"Caroline" wouldn't leave her tipi*
> *for a house on the reserve.*

One day some men came.

Grandma Caroline was sitting in a rocking chair
in front of her tipi. Smoking her pipe.

The men picked her up, chair and all,
put her in a house on the reserve.

Grandma held on
to her pipe and her rocking chair and
swore at the men as they carried her away.

SUBJECT: MISSING FATHERS

From: jbrass@hall.com
To: miwama@hotmail.com

dad got a letter from vital statistics. they have no record of his birth.

in a way i think he's happy his orphan story is proved right.

still won't talk about mary being his mother though.

love,
janis

From: miwama@hotmail.com
To: jbrass@hall.com

what a shame, i'm sorry we started all this.

mom was positively giddy about surprising her little brother with his birth certificate. now they don't even have a record?

how can it be?
m

ONE LITTLE TWO LITTLE

i

The Honourable
  The Minister of the Interior:

Sir, we're doing our best here to decide
who's Indian, so we can get Treaty 4 signed.

Some of these people have white fathers
but live on the reserve like Indians. Most

of the Indians say those ones are Indians.
A few of the ones we think are Indians live

in town with the white folk. Lots of Halfbreeds
live like white men, even if Section 31 says they're Indian.

Not everyone wants the five dollars.
Is there any advice you might give us?

> We have the honour to be, Sir,
>   Your obedient servants,
>   W.J. CHRISTIE,
>   *Indian Commissioner.*
>   M.G. DICKIESON.

ii

Messrs. Christie and Dickieson:

Don't let the dark ones fool you.

Sincerely,
Your Honourable Minister

SCRIP APPLICATION

"I was born in St. Andrews, Manitoba, in 1841,"
someone says for Grandma Caroline.
Someone listens to her Cree and says,

"I lived in Manitoba. Then I came with my parents
to the North-West Territories." Someone

bends toward Grandma Caroline
around the edge of her kerchief
to lips waiting for the pipe
she cradles in her pocket. Bends

the sound Grandma Caroline manages in that room.

"I lived in Manitoba to the year 1860
when I came with my parents to Old Wives Lake . . . "

   the company men called it dead sea country for the salt

  you ever see the birds at old wives lake?

   pelicans ducks geese plovers

one day their headman shot a pelican
    just so he could stretch the wings

      he wouldn't believe a bird could reach

    wider than him

Someone reminds Grandma Caroline why
she's in that office.
Explains to the one writing:
"She's an old woman. It takes her a long time."

"Yes, I lived at Old Wives Lake and in ceded territory ever
since . . . "

> *married?   ka kihci wîkihtohk?*
> *husband . . . awîyak onâpima*
>
> *oh — niwîkimâkan*

"Yes, two of them: Charles Bird and Baptiste Pelletier . . . "

> *and willie kennedy   at fort qu'appelle*
> *ever hear about willie? he had the same job as you*
> *listen*
>
> *and tell them what they want to hear*

"Her children," he lies.
"She's remembering their mischief."
And scolds her. Yes,

he'd heard stories about Willie,
how Willie used to string the factor along,
the governor even.

About the pretty girl
who lived with her folks at the Fort.
She disappeared, they said.
There might have been a baby.

The soft *ts-ts* of Grandma's tongue against her teeth.

SUBJECT: LAST NIGHT'S DREAM

From: jbrass@hall.com
To: miwama@hotmail.com

hi. so we're visiting sarah at peepeekisis, she has things to show me, tell me. you and clo are there. and dad, looking like my ex — how freudian can you get! all three of you are tall and thin.

while i'm talking to sarah and her adopted daughter you all go out to swim in the lake. I warn you: "hey you guys, don't go too deep! why aren't you wearing any clothes?"

you call back: "we're on our own reserve — we don't need clothes."

i'm the only one who cares you're naked.

how about that?
janis

From: miwama@hotmail.com
To: jbrass@hall.com

so — were uncle bud and clo and i sarah's "show and tell"? you gotta think about this. why us? why tall and thin? and naked?

are the three of us diving into the "waters of remembrance"?

is it time for you to join us?

what important thing does sarah have to teach us? is the adopted daughter saying something about blood? about acceptance?

i think it's a big one.

see you,
m

HOMESICK

i

home from camping
you smell Mom says
like you just came off the reserve
we laugh

ii

I learn the word racism
decide Mom's racist
for what she said
me, too, for laughing

iii

I find out Mom's Indian
remember her saying how I smelled
like the reserve
maybe she was just homesick

SUBJECT: APOLOGY

From: miwama@hotmail.com
To: jbrass@hall.com

got a letter from my church about the need to apologize for
the pain and suffering caused by its "involvement" in the
indian residential school system, that we all bear "blessings"
and "burdens" from our ancestors.

no kidding.

as a member of the church, i'm supposed to join them on
"the road of repentance, reconciliation and healing."

what if i'm not ready to accept an apology from me?

m

From: jbrass@hall.com
To: miwama@hotmail.com

i don't know what to tell you.

i spoke to dad yesterday. he finally admitted he's metis,
then wanted to know what I thought about that — did i hate
him for it?

i asked him if people called him a half-breed. he said they
called him that and worse. said the hardest thing was when
boys he thought were his friends would be vicious towards
him. like the time doc kitley's kid beat him with a baseball bat.
that all he could do was cry.

i said auntie colleen has no recollection of other boys beating
him up. he never told anyone — what could they do?

janis

AFTER HEARING "IT CROSSES MY MIND"
for Marilyn Dumont

I heard you read at the university:

      pass me the bannock like it's mine

heard you read about a girl

      whose mother is Metis but
      only half as Metis as her grandmother,
      what will she name herself

And it came to me:
Mom married white and I'm
proof.

The next day was my turn.
I mumbled *maybe I study*
my sons' Asian history
to brown up my own.

Because, I might have said,
shame swallowed my past
sucked it out of my mother's mouth
emptied her head of it, even.

The crowd shifted
looked down.

I ran to where I could
turn the waterworks on full blast.
Like Dad would tease.

And kept right on running,
on the lookout
for bannock and tea.

FAMILY TRAIT

I turn around on the path. Head back
past the point where I can say *here is where*

*I had my first kiss. Here is where I was five
and hid behind the door. Look! Here's my wagon,*

*my brother's tricycle, the blue hood of my carriage
where I slept on the porch in winter.*

Back to a place where I only hear things, like I hear
Caroline had a baby she gave to the Bourassas

over at Pasquah. And Mary had two babies
she left with her mother. And Mary's sister had a baby

who disappeared, and then she had Eunice, too —
both of them before she married Mr. Feindt. And I hear

Eunice had Rose before she married Mr. Seymour
but she called her Rose Seymour anyway.

And Mary's other sister had a baby before she married
Mr. Graham. And most of them still alive are kind of shocked

when they hear about the others, especially if I tell them
out of the blue like that or let on I know.

Ask them what do they think about sharing babies?
About so many women in our family having babies

and then marrying, ever since the old days. Do they suppose
it's a family trait, like diabetes? Cousin Roy figures

*Cree women are just so damn beautiful white guys
never could keep their hands off them. What did I expect?*

I dunno I tell him. *But I hear some of the women
aren't real happy about the whole thing.*

SUBJECT: BELONGING

From: miwama@hotmail.com
To: jbrass@hall.com
Attachments: A/b Colloq.doc (54KB)

well cousin, here's a copy of my first coming out. what a day.

it was a colloquium on "aboriginal autobiography." I DIDN'T CRY.

alannah's helped me find so many ways of dealing with all this
that i just imagined the hill by the little red river (bella's hill?).
big sky, big view, helper wolf beside me.

i'm always so not-quite-in with every group i know — even my
own family. but on that hill I BELONG.

don't worry, not asking you to get your feet wet or anything.
notice i didn't even hint about you in it?

much, much love
m

_____

From: jbrass@hall.com
To: miwama@hotmail.com

you're doing interesting things. i'm scared to.
i did work on the old genealogy bit the other night.

i don't feel indian, in fact i'm just starting to be able to say
"first nations". i like to tell people i'm indian, just as i say that i
like metallica. to shock them. maybe it's a way to rationalize
not belonging.

i think i have stereotypes that need to be cleared from my
head, ghostly ones that i wasn't even aware of. when i start
classes next fall, i'll try and visit the longhouse. maybe even go
talk things over with alannah.

love,
your cowardly cousin

FOR SHAME

these mothers lie
pinned to the earth
by the weight of stones:

    bastard indian, you know

        took her in   not her real mother
can't be a breed   look how pretty
             she is   c'mon pretty squaw
    give you a good time   every time
  I climbed that
      hill behind
         the school so lonely   the nuns

      couldn't find me   like the only one

one by one
daughters lift the stones
show the world

and the mothers lie still
unable to bear
their absence

SUBJECT: CONFIRMATION

From: jbrass@hall.com
To: miwama@hotmail.com

am i ever glad we finally tracked kay down. imagine her and your mom being such close cousins and your mom not seeing her for all these years. i know — it makes sense. our parents couldn't have denied the past like they did without cutting themselves off from everyone. but still . . . it's just so sad.

last time we were on the phone, i asked kay if mary really was our parents' parent. i threw her with such a bald question, but it was burning inside me. she said at first that she assumed it, then she said that bella referred to our parents as "mary's kids."

she also said bella's first husband, mr. linklater, was very good to her, but life was rough with william caldwell.

love,
janis

A GRANDMOTHER SPELL FOR MAKING HER YOURS

spin around ten times
eyes closed

clap your hands
twice shout *Nôhkom*

loud as three crows
in the winter poplars

if the spell doesn't take at first
keep spinning

BELLA'S HOUSE

Auntie Kay says Grandma Bella was a strong woman,
strong enough to have sixteen children
and keep half of them alive.

She knew hard times with that husband of hers,
William Caldwell, the carpenter.
He built furniture and houses all around the county.

But not for Bella.
Oh no, she had to live in that old shack.
Hunt and trap just to keep food on the table.

One day she sat in the kitchen praying her heart out:
Oh Lord, get that man to fix this house. And if a chunk of
ceiling didn't fall on her head, right then and there.

After that, Grandpa William didn't have a choice.
He built Grandma a new house, big enough
for all their kids, and Auntie Kay and her mom and sisters

and Clem and Eunice and all the others who came along.
Grandpa died in that house the year before the war ended.
Grandma wouldn't die for almost ten more years,

not until Mom married a good man and had her first baby.
That's the house there in this photograph. And there's Mom
and Uncle Bud on the front step, laughing.

From: miwama@hotmail.com
To: jbrass@hall.com

sure would like to know how bella and mary thought of themselves. the men too, outside of whatever the census said.

did they call themselves, imagine themselves, one thing or another?

got all choked when i had buffy st. marie playing today. it's like something's trying to get out of me — like labour pains and pushing with no baby. but that's too easy, because the feeling is usually out of my eyes and mouth, like something's trying to get in too.

am i going crazy?

love,
m

From: jbrass@hall.com
To: miwama@hotmail.com

there was an orphanage in lestock that took indian children in. what if mary wasn't their mother and bella just got them from the orphanage? or what if she was their mother and tried to give them up and bella wouldn't let her?

i wonder what they called themselves too. just know my dad didn't call himself indian . . .

i've stopped saying that i'm metis. i say that i'm half-breed or that i'm indian and mennonite. when i finished maria campbell's book today i put cher on. "*half-breed*, how i learned to hate the word." was in tears listening to that one.

at least you're not going crazy alone.

janis

CRADLESONG

My mother taught me how to make an Indian cradle.
I remembered last Thursday in Doull's Books
over a secondhand version of *The Art of Allen Sapp*.

Clo said I might like his stuff, that he was from around home,
from Red Pheasant. I noticed how dark he paints these scenes
I've read about: making rabbit soup, tending bannock on the fire,

pounding chokecherries . . . *layered them with lard and stored them
in gunnysacks*, Auntie Kay explains, *for the winter*. Heard about.

An old woman, a lamp. And in one shadowed corner
of his grandmother's cabin, he paints a cradle I know,
and one in the tipi, and another, and another, and . . .

my mother's dark hair soft on my arm, showing me
how to rock my doll. *There you go — back and forth
back and forth* . . .

Rock skitters down the riverbank.

> *You taught me how to make a cradle!*

>> *Sigh.*

> *How did you know?*

>> *Mom must have shown me.*

> *Grandma Bella?*

>> *Mm-hm . . . yes, they must have rocked their babies in them.*

IT MATTERS

what *are* you?
you're my own sweet boy

                  c'mon you know what I mean

you're Superman saving the world
in your ratty red and blue pyjamas

                  Mo-om

okay, you're Robin Hood stealing money from the rich guys
so we can get a break from beans and rice

                  what do I say when they ask?

say . . .
I'm whoever I want to be   just like you

                  that's not what they wanna know

it doesn't matter what they want, it's what you want

                  it matters

okay it matters   say   *you first*

                  lame   I can see what they are

okay   say they're being rude and it's none of their business

                  you want me to get beat up?

SUBJECT: MARY IN THE MIDDLE

From: miwama@hotmail.com
To: jbrass@hall.com

sorry i messed up about finding grandma bella's school records.

i wrote mary a letter yesterday afternoon, mostly about being angry with mom. then i dreamed about mary.

she was all soft and dark and had circles under her eyes — just like our folks. mary and mom and uncle bud were sitting on the couch, mary in the middle. she told them to grow up and stop acting like kids. she was so funny. that's all i remember.

much love,
marilyn

From: jbrass@hall.com
To: miwama@hotmail.com

wow, you even worry more than me about offending the other person! you didn't do ANYTHING to screw up.

i think i'm less emotionally attached to these people. they are my relatives, but i don't particularly want to meet them and talk to them — the dead ones, that is — like you do. i just want to know why they did the things they did.

i haven't really said these things before, maybe *i* should apologize.

love,
janis

MEETING GRANDMA

lupine, peony — the ones I love

best and least together
beside Grandma Mary's grave

three green durum fields
highway arcing by

moon glow
and the old couple

strolling row by row

THIS MIGHT BE ALL ABOUT LOVE

Today on the phone I tried again to tell you
I know how it hurts when children refuse
the gifts mothers give in love. I planned it all out.
I'd mention Adam, how he doubts
my best intentions. Tie that in
to my birth certificate, how it says you were
an Irish orphan. Maybe you wrote that
way back when so your daughter
wouldn't be Indian.
Too bad she didn't have the decency
to be grateful. I'd say

I know how that response could hurt
someone who intended love. Then I'd shift
to other histories of fear and ignorance
how the thorns of colonization petrify
in the hearts of its Natives and how absolutely
torn a mother would be to turn from her family
and orphan her kids along with herself
by wrapping them all in the right side of the blanket.

But that might sound cruel.
And if Dad ever heard . . .

Dad — always the first
to spot *those Indians*

slouching on the viaduct or
tossed out the door of the Avenue Hotel.

SUBJECT: ANOTHER MEETING

From: miwama@hotmail.com
To: jbrass@hall.com

so that's cousin edna. has she been through the mill. imagine being one of only 4 kids left out of 17. murders, suicides, o.d.s, alcohol — the whole ugly rainbow.

she's only one year older than me, you know. i can't believe we grew up in the same town — me breezing through public school the whole time she's up the hill in residential school. we both came to vancouver in '75.

and edna's brother in the pen. do you suppose dad knew, working there? i'll check the dates. all those injuries on the autopsy — and the bottom line: death from "natural causes."

the same old crap.

i think you were out of the room when edna invited us to the mother's day powwow at trout lake. want to come? she said she'd introduce us around.

can you believe we laughed so much?

m

PROPER SAD

they say Grandma Mary said nothing
when she heard her father'd died

just turned to the wood box
and quietly wept

shed tears they said
as if tears could

wait like leaves or skin
for some whispered yes

like children
hugging the horizon

silent
with consent

SUBJECT: POWWOW

From: miwama@hotmail.com
To: jbrass@hall.com

the best thing was actually sitting there with family instead of being another one of the wannabes. edna seemed just as proud to introduce me to her friends and family as i was proud to introduce her to mine. yes, some of my friends were there, if no other family. sorry — cheap shot.

edna looked beautiful. did you know her old man was haida? she was wearing black pants and white shirt with a black and red haida vest.

i danced one of the intertribals — long after edna started asking me.

it was tough seeing the evidence of hard living on so many of the people. that in-your-face reminder of another part of our heritage.

i love the way edna explained to people how it was our whole family that was broken up, not just that mom and uncle bud cut themselves off from everyone.

maybe you'll come next time. no pressure, though,

m

THE LOVELIEST INDIAN

T.B. I laugh. It's a joke:
I've been sitting so long, I have T.B.
The joke wears out like our tired bottoms.
Not like my cousin, who got T.B. from sharing
a bed with Auntie Nellie.

There are two pictures of Nellie,
one shot in a field of grass.
Nellie stands beside Mrs. Ross,
who is wearing her Salvation
Army uniform. Mrs. Ross and the League of Mercy
will visit Nellie every week in The San.
Reason enough for Mrs. Ross's face to beam
beside Nellie's in the iron bed. In that one,

Nellie's eyes are big and round as saucers —
something Mrs. Ross, acquainted with teas and bazaars,
might say. *She was the loveliest Indian girl*
with eyes as big as saucers, especially
after she lost all her weight. I agree.
Nellie looks Indian. Punjabi even,
her cheeks pale beneath black brows, dark eyes
drawn by the weight of bleached pillowslips.

We find Nellie on the outskirts of town,
lying next to Olga Buchinsky, a good
mile or so from the others: *Nellie Brass*
1913–37   In Loving Memory.

SUBJECT: TWO WORLDS, ONE BODY

From: miwama@hotmail.com
To: jbrass@hall.com

here we go — our first official collaboration! imagine sitting through a whole conference on aboriginal/mennonite relations and not hearing one paper on intermarriage. talk about right place, right time.

are you okay with the "conversation" format? we can keep on emailing as usual, but sharpen the focus for a while, talk more about all these marriages we've been finding out about — latest count is 25 in our family alone, right?

stuff like: why abo/menno? why so many in our family? AND why doesn't anyone talk/write about it?

don't be nervous, okay? i know you're just starting with this university business, but we can do it. i've got a little experience, you've got a lot of determination.

yay us,
m

From: jbrass@hall.com
To: miwama@hotmail.com

sounds good to me. my head hurts this weekend from just trying to understand academic writing. but i do think we need to talk about dad and auntie colleen and their mother each marrying mennonites, without the others knowing.

oh, guess what? after all that maria campbell said at the conference about *peace shall destroy many*, i went out and got it. rudy wiebe was writing about our folks ages ago — intermarriage, shame, all of it!

it made me think of when we lived up island. i identified myself as an "Indian" even though my father didn't. even though other half-breed children I knew didn't call themselves "indian". but i was ashamed of being "indian" whenever we went to port hardy and saw what it could mean.

i'm beginning to understand what kept our folks quiet.

oh, who am i trying to kid? i'm terrified about writing this paper. really and truly terrified. i don't know enough, i'm not smart enough, i don't know how to write, i just don't know.

help,
janis

GRANDMOTHER CUP

Nôhkom's blue and white polka dot teacup
rim toothed with etchings
cracks and chips
worn smooth by lips
that drink sweet tea
with every meal and more —

Nôhkom's old cracked cup is mine now
I call it *teacup*   *chyawan*   *minihkwâcikan*   call it grazing
on glossal possibilities   call it lapping up the lingua of my francas

sip

minihkwâcikan *n. Cree*   teacup
chyawan *n. Japanese*   1. rice bowl
                              2. tea cup

    (imagine the conversation with Grossma!)
        Drinkje en äte?
        Yes, the same word.
        No, not rice from a teacup but
        sometimes tea from a rice bowl).

                swish

my teacup   *watashi no chyawan*
my teacup   *ninihkwâcikan*

                        swallow

with this spotted this bulging this brindled —

        tongues
        hot on this tongue
        burning long, this night
        of longing

SUBJECT: PRIDE

From: miwama@hotmail.com
To: jbrass@hall.com

just finished re-reading *april raintree.* man that book can pull
you down. this time i saw mom in cheryl as she meets her
"gutter-life" father for the first time. imagined mom imagining
such a meeting. keeping us from it, with love.

just when i start feeling sympathy and more understanding,
the "yes, but" comes creeping back. where did i learn to be so
judgmental?

it's not a great day for being indian.

then i think how easy it is for me to slip into the woodwork
and just do an april. i'm not liking writing this essay today.
m

From: jbrass@hall.com
To: miwama@hotmail.com

"all will be well, all will be well, all manner of things will be well."

yes, we are like our parents. we just each have our own ways of
coping with our lot.

your mom's denial and turning her back on her past have
given you the opportunity to learn and accomplish all that you
have. because of this, it's easier for us to look at our history.
and it's helping SO MANY PEOPLE in our family.

your mom is not cheryl or april or maria. she had a
mother/grandmother who loved her, a home, an identity.
if you have to read, re-read our email: see the anger and the
sadness that we have been through to get this far. and boy,
have we come far!

you love your mom and she loves you.

ponderous and heavy message over,
janis

WINTER SHEETS

The old woman in black
came to my sister Sunday night
twisting knotted fingers.
Angry. Clo had moved her bed
and the woman couldn't reach it anymore.
I know what it's about Clo said.
Insanity. I couldn't stop her.
I tried.

And I saw the tangled fingers
dragging fear through bulging knuckles
like Mom did
sheets on washday
foam dammed against the wringer
catch your hair if you're not careful
flattened wrinkles frozen on the line
sheets walked in at noon
stood in the basement corner
for their own good
to thaw.

Winter sheets smelling spring.

Monday night the woman came
to me and I screamed *NO.*
Crazy sisters I agreed.

Tuesday morning telephone.
My mother's words.
The other sister . . . whose husband
found her in the bed. Said
she wouldn't answer and
the smell of the sheets was . . . wrong.

WAITING FOR SONG

because the wind already speaks
a thousand tongues

licking ruddy calves that climb
a hill blue with the smell of hot sage

trailing petals across her round belly
white in moon's full light

fingering each scar

SUBJECT: REV. MATTHEWS

From: jbrass@hall.com
To: miwama@hotmail.com

he wanted to know if you were open-minded about residential schools. turns out he ran two and worked at another.

he has strong views, said that all are being sullied by a few people, that he sincerely loves indian children like his own.

i assured him you were a lovely person with the most open mind ever. we didn't get an invitation to stay there, but he will meet us at the church.

good night,
janis

ROAD SIGNS

July afternoon on the Number 8
heat snakes free of the disappearing road
vies for the horizon with canola yellow
leafcutter bees
tumble into cups of blue flax

Grossma's tidy prairie table
                    where we hunt
            lost
      for that place
                    where   the other grandmother
                joined
      here with *there*

that bend in the river
that swallows Qu'Appelle
where east flows back
and we are compelled
                    here   elbow of the Assiniboine

            Assiniboine?
            near Carry the Kettle
            you can't miss it

                    we miss it and miss it   until
                    at the corner of our eyes
                    hawk flies
                    alongside

            turns
            we follow
      turns and . . .
                    there
                          where willow sweeps the bank

THINGS MY GROSSMA TAUGHT ME

summer borscht is different
than winter borscht

porridge tastes better
on toast

always take special care
of the good china

grace is best
in High German

SKIN WHISPERS DOWN

you're scouring my skin with your looking
thin sheets whisper to the floor

go ahead   pick a sheet up   hold it
carry it to the window

where fog linens the light wide
hold it up to the glass   sheet on bleary sheet

you might read whorls and furrows
might see   patterns in the curving here
or there   *ah   that explains it*

if the meager light distracts you
try stroking my skin   yes

your finger's dull in the foggy haze
the sheet flimsy and worn

even so   you might feel the crease of a reason
might decide   that is me and this is why

HOSPITAL *GLORY*
for Sumie and Atsushi Ishimatsu

I try to pray for Sumie
that her leaving would lighten.
Try a sentence about her pain
her husband   children
watching her.
Please don't come she tells them
konai de.

I whisper her name and see
something like Sumie
bruised skin blurring the pin tips of her
thin bones   dark smudge of her eyes
in the wings of an eagle
carried high.

*

I wait for Atsushi to call.
Friends are asking
how I could think Sumie's gone.
Why not look on the bright side?
Yes   you've lost a few people in the last while
but why borrow trouble?

*

Atsushi calls. Sumie is alive.
Free of pain. *More or less*
under control.

*

But the eagle . . .
the body lifted up . . .
who is left in that bed
in the hospital called *Glory?*
That space staked out for pain
like the garden row called *feverfew.*

SUBJECT: REPETITION

From: jbrass@hall.com
To: miwama@hotmail.com

sure felt like last night's class was all about our family. the silencing of language, the shame, the secrets. i had it all figured out during class, but i'm exhausted these days and my thoughts are not working as they should.

i'll wait 'til the weekend.

janis

_____

From: miwama@hotmail.com
To: jbrass@hall.com

exactly — the class, the movie, the conversation, whatever it is, somebody says it's about something else but the arrows come right at you, don't they? you know they really mean you, but there's the difference.

this is not the "all about you" kind of "you", but what they did to you/your family, what your history is, the history of an entire people, a project of genocide and "you" bear the scars, the fruit . . .

don't kill yourself trying to figure it out. it's a chimera, a pale curtain, a guillotine, a "healing" hand, an answer, a question.

"IT" is everything and it changes and escapes and there's no figuring, i figure.

much love,
m

THE SCATTERING

Once the younger sister
is finally blessed
the older sister writes:

> *Her ashes didn't look like ashes,*
> *more like broken bits of shell*
> *washed up on a shore,*
> *many more than a pretty urn's worth.*
>
> *And the dust from these ashes*
> *is carried by the wind*
> *and caught by the skin*
> *of my daughter's suntanned arms.*

One day soon
the daughter talks
about blue jay babies
and in days her story dwindles
to the one who couldn't fly,
how she found it by the tree.

And her brown hands fashion
a cross and invitations
to a blue jay funeral:

> *R.S.V.P. and kindly say a few words.*
> *This is the kind of bird she was:*

What words are there for
a bird who never learned to fly
who died two days into summer . . .

A JOB FOR GOD

You can't wear a rhinestone jacket
to your mother's funeral I tell my niece.

She pirouettes in the three-way mirror.
Tests the swirl of black beneath glitter.

Yes. It'll be perfect
for the dance next week.
Save it.

One dress for dancing and mourning. But I
draw the line at rhinestones for a funeral.
Especially your mother's, when you're twelve.

This is a pagan decision.
I am not claiming God's promise
that mourning will turn to dancing.
Not surprising, since our church forbids dancing
and the taking of one's own life —
that's a job for God.

Our grief doesn't qualify for transformation.
We will always mourn.
The wages of my sister's sin.

I get back at God a few months later
when I choose another outfit for my niece:
blue jeans and her pink sequined T-shirt
to wear tomorrow in her own coffin.

I'm not convinced God's impressed
but I like to think my niece cares.

SUBJECT: JUST WONDERING

From miwama@hotmail.com
To: jbrass@hall.com

do you ever FEEL anything other than white?

has anything changed for you inside? not just about what you know now, but what it makes you?

does that knowledge make you something different in your own heart and mind, or just in how others make you out to be, given what name you tell them?

love,
m

From: jbrass@hall.com
To: miwama@hotmail.com

do I feel other than white? i'd say no. i now identify with aboriginal people that i see on the streets. i think, "hey brother, sister." but then i worry that i am appropriating their identity. i have no idea what they have lived through.

on the few occasions that i joined edna in groups that were overwhelmingly aboriginal, i felt white — and an outsider.

growing up in gimli, there were many native families. i never spoke to them and was a silent witness to the name-calling. i was afraid those white kids would find out that i had native blood and then ostracize me.

when i was working on the oil rigs i was showing photographs of my friends to some of the workers. they looked at my friend janet and her two kids and laughed and asked who those "wagon-burners" were. i got angry but never told them i was a wagon-burner too.

love,
janis

GETTING OVER IT

find words large enough to hold the dead
— Lorna Crozier

What can you say
when the knocking comes hard
and too soon and in a second
there's no imagining
the one who answered? Before

I thought her name
and there she was. Now
paraffinned orange in a box.
Death begs conjuring

the way she looked that Christmas
not the one her eyes wouldn't hold
and her head slumped onto the plate
in spite of our talking fast and loud

begs forgetting
last spring's ghost skin
the time
it wasn't enough
to vacuum her stomach dry
and we bartered for days
with mechanical breaths   until
she came back
for a while. Now
we're sorting through
words that might hold her

marking time with her absence
a week today we say
it's been a month already   two   blink
and the road disappears.

SUBJECT: THE BIG LEAP

From: jbrass@hall.com
To: miwama@hotmail.com

i'm applying for status. i've collected everything together, i'm taking two more applications up to courtenay with me next weekend and i'm signing my brothers up at the same time. i've told them NOT TO SAY ANYTHING to dad!

unfortunately they may have to ask mom for their long form birth certificates and if they tell her, she will tell dad.

what do you think?

janis

The girl reaches into the linen closet for the plastic
grocery bag. Empties out a checked apron
and fuchsia housecoat. Burrows her nose in old cloth.

When she got the clothes they smelled of tobacco smoke.
I haven't washed them her auntie said in a kind of apology —
it's what she was wearing when she passed.

Now the girl smells sage — from the time she wore the house
coat while she prayed. It's the first of May and cool.
She puts the housecoat on again,

lays the apron on her desk. Smoothes the wrinkles. How
could she have missed that cigarette burn just above
the hem? The handkerchief still bunched

in the apron pocket: blue morning glories, pink
bluebells, yellow lily-of-the-valley. The girl had decided
the orange check of the apron clashed with fuchsia.

But I don't know she thinks now. *With that mauve in the check
it almost goes.* She considers wearing
the housecoat. Leaving it on while she cooks or

does the laundry. Considers a beer on the couch
in the fuchsia housecoat and checked apron.
A cigarette even. How it might feel

the next time she says *All my Relations.*
Fake she decides. She folds the apron and housecoat
once more. Returns the bag to its shelf.

GRANNIE LOVED HER KIDS

Remember how you imagined you were an Indian
princess then Jewish when you heard about
those Brasses from Israel how I joked
compared to the others I must be

adopted and we hit the road looking
for some beginning a name
our graveyard kit with the whisk broom
and scissors for hacking at weeds in case

one headstone might say *here's your grandfather* or someone
on the reserve — Sarah or Gladys or Ivor —
would remember *sure I knew your grandpa*
he was a good man he and your grannie

just couldn't make a go of it or he died real young
your grannie loved her kids so much
she gave them to her folks how
we keep finding Brasses in the archives

some of them look like us especially
around the belly and you say
there's a Brass for you
every time we apologize

for imposing or don't phone in case
the other one might be doing something
important or we do and you say
can you believe my dad he said

keep that woman away from me she's no sister of mine
and we have a big laugh over that one
tears jumping off our cheekbones and in between the heaves
I say *no way you know what Mom says those*

Aboriginals have nothing to do with me
what now?

THE EARTH IT CARRIES

This rock comes from the North Saskatchewan.
One summer. Home for no sad reason. I'm free
on my walks along the river to look.

I don't use the walk to escape planning a funeral,
getting someone into hospital or out of it.
Waiting for them to wake up.

Birds on the sandbar at the foot of 15th Avenue.
The river is so wide I can't see
to name them. White birds and dark.
Maybe gulls or ducks. Geese,
if it's not too early. And plovers?

When I was young I never asked the name
of this bird or that rock. At least I don't remember asking.
You'd think I'd remember.

If my son asked I would say *this is sandstone,*
smooth and round from tumbling over rocks.
Brown like the earth it carries. I'd say
the shiny white bits are Columbian quartz.

And the tiny circles, like someone strong
poked it with a straw? he'd ask. *What are they?*

DREAMING NAMES

We travel to a naming ceremony.
In a wagon train, a line of cars
driving to the naming.

I do something wrong. Something
they laugh at. Because it's wrong.
I forget what it is. Alannah's there

explaining so I'll understand
and learn. Quietly, like she does
in her office. There's a list —

names to be given, four or five. I can't
remember the names. I knew them once.
I don't even know who gets the names. There are

so many people. Together in a room.
We camp one night on the way. That's when
the elders laugh at the thing I do.

SUBJECT: INDIANS

From: jbrass@hall.com
To: miwama@hotmail.com

i got the word via a telephone call this morning — i'm not
an indian, neither are doug and james. we're metis. it all
hinges on the fact that peter, william caldwell, bella et al. took
scrip.

oh well. i am at peace with this decision. what have i
experienced of the "indian" and reserve life? i still feel like
i was trying to co-opt their history.

we've got howard adams and maria campbell!

janis

SKY TALK

When the dream ends
and the siren continues
I search the sky for fire.
Find only stars. Bewildered

I wrap my shivering body in a blanket
step out the back door
and sit on the stoop
at the edge of this valley.

Northern lights are slow dancing
with the great bear. Draping modest hunters
in suckling green.

At home I would drop my blanket
and light emerald   crimson   white
would wrap me as it does
any body that interrupts the night sky.

And I would lay mine down
on the dew-soft sage
beneath the hunters and the bear.

Drink deep. Wait
while cool fingers trace
the trail of our longing.